Rewiring Your Personality

Unveiling Practical Techniques to Break Free from Narcissistic Traits and Create Meaningful Connections

Joseph S dinger

copyright © (Joseph S. Dinger) (2024)

Table of Contents

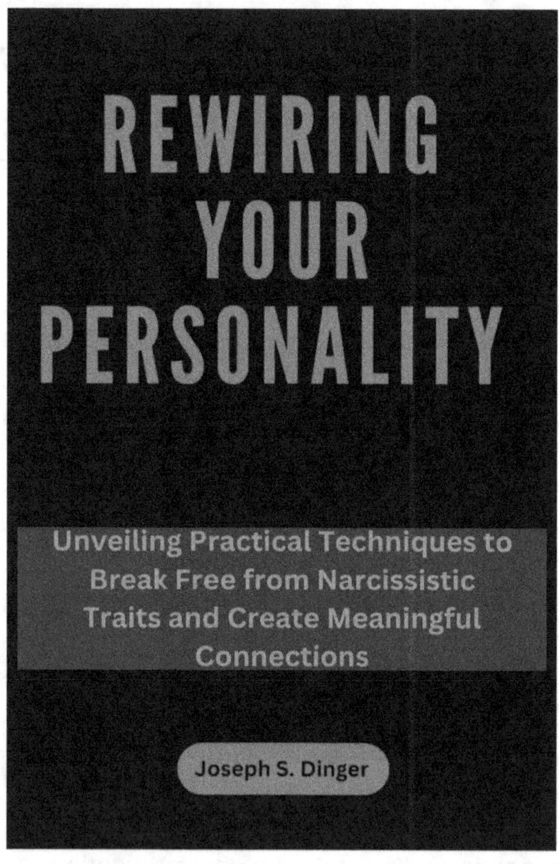
REWIRING
YOUR
PERSONALITY
Unveiling Practical Techniques to Break Free from Narcissistic Traits and Create Meaningful Connections
Joseph S. Dinger

Chapter 1: Understanding Narcissism

Recognizing Narcissistic Traits: Identifying behaviors that may reflect narcissistic tendencies.

I was sucked into a vicious cycle of self-indulgence and didn't realize how it affected my relationships or my own development. It was only at a turning point that I realized how some actions were a reflection of narcissistic tendencies, which prevented me from seeing real relationships.

As my close friend Sarah talked about her challenges, I found myself thinking more about my own successes and accomplishments. Rather than expressing empathy, I found myself trying to outdo her experiences by bringing the subject back to my own life.

Sarah's observation that "it feels like you're not really listening" struck a chord with me at that moment. I realized that my inclination to center conversations around myself, minimize the feelings of others, and relentlessly pursue approval were characteristics of narcissism.

As I gave it more thought, I saw patterns of entitlement in my behavior. I frequently assumed I should be given preference over other people and expected to be treated better. Whether I was demanding special treatment or making my ideas known during conversations, I was obliging and I didn't realize the consequences.

Moreover, the constant desire for recognition had turned into a motivating factor. Seeking recognition from others made it difficult for me to see the fundamental worth of what I did. It was getting worrying that she was always looking for compliments and that she felt empty when they weren't given.

This was a freeing yet unpleasant understanding. These actions weren't just defects; rather, they were manifestations of more profound fears. To deal with them required a conscious change in attitude and conduct.

I set out on a self-reflection trip to address these tendencies. I deliberately steered the discourse away from myself by engaging in active listening. Journaling and other introspective activities were helpful in identifying the fears that were causing me to become narcissistic.

In addition, accepting humility served as my compass. Real connections were created by appreciating the perspectives and experiences of others and by embracing vulnerability as a strength. I progressively shifted my focus from pursuing outside approval to cultivating internal fulfillment in my deeds.

Recognizing and naming these actions was the first step. To face them and make the decision to change required guts. I've begun releasing myself from the bonds of narcissistic inclinations through self-awareness and deliberate efforts, promoting real connections and personal development.

Understanding the Impact: Exploring how narcissistic traits affect personal relationships and self-growth.

Periods of detachment dogged my life, a result of unresolved narcissistic tendencies that unintentionally hampered my emotional connections and impeded my personal development.

My relationships were where the first signs of the harm these characteristics caused to appear. Emily, my partner, frequently complained about feeling ignored in talks. I didn't really connect with her ideas and feelings since I kept directing conversations toward my goals or successes. Our relationship's basis was gradually undermined by this lack of real connection, which resulted in increasing emotional distance and discord.

Friendships also took the brunt of my narcissistic conduct, outside of sexual relationships. I came to the realization that my self-centered chats and continual demand for approval had made close friends uncomfortable. They progressively drifted away as I failed to realize the toll my actions had put on our relationships because they felt ignored and unappreciated.

It had an effect that went beyond interpersonal interactions; it was a roadblock to personal development. My conceit made it difficult for me to be open to criticism. I missed opportunities for growth and learning because I saw constructive criticism as an attack on my ego rather than as a way to get better.

Moreover, this conduct hindered my capacity to establish significant relationships in work environments. My emphasis on promoting myself took precedence over teamwork, impeding both mutual development and teamwork. Coworkers experienced alienation, which had an impact on the cohesiveness of the team as well as my productivity.

An important turning point came when these implications were realized. It was a painful awakening that made me reflect deeply on how my behaviors affected my relationships and my own growth.

I started a journey to become more self-aware, reading books on emotional intelligence and going to counseling to address these characteristics. I have learned the value of active listening and the depth of empathy as a result of this experience. I discovered how to turn my attention away from myself and develop a sincere curiosity in the thoughts and feelings of others.

Embracing my vulnerability turned into my superpower. I began owning up to my errors and being vulnerable in public, which led to the development of stronger bonds based on sincerity and trust. Relationships started to heal gradually as I fostered an atmosphere that encouraged respect and understanding between people. This was not an easy transformation, nor was it quick. It required self-reflection, perseverance, and a readiness to accept discomfort. But as I worked to overcome these narcissistic tendencies, I saw my own development materialize right before my eyes.

I started to be more receptive to criticism and saw it as a tool for growth rather than an attack on who I was. This increased openness to myself drove me to keep improving and to have a deeper comprehension of my advantages and disadvantages.

In summary, narcissism had a knock-on effect that affected every aspect of my life, preventing personal development and sabotaging relationships. However, by reflecting, being committed, and being open to change, I've begun to mend those breaks and open doors to personal growth that were previously firmly closed.

REWIRING YOUR PERSONALITY

Unveiling Practical Techniques to Break Free from Narcissistic Traits and Create Meaningful Connections

Joseph S. Dinger

Chapter 2: The Journey Within

Self-Reflection and Awareness: Techniques to introspect and understand your own behavior and its impact.

My narcissistic inclinations had a major impact on my relationships and personal growth, and realizing this led me on a transformative journey of self-discovery and introspection.

Writing in my journal became my haven, a secure place where I could process the complexity of my feelings and ideas. Every post was an unfiltered investigation of the underlying reasons for my actions. As I spilled my guts on the paper, themes began to show themselves. My deep-seated desire for approval from others, times of uncertainty, and fear of inadequacy started to become apparent to me as recurrent triggers for my self-centeredness.

Counseling sessions also turned into a crucial component of my self-discovery process. I was able to reveal previously hidden levels of feelings and mental processes through facilitated talks and activities. My therapist guided me through the maze of my own mind with a combination of perceptive questioning and compassionate probing, which helped me see where my narcissistic tendencies stemmed from—past experiences and unfulfilled emotional needs.

I found that mindfulness meditation was an effective technique for objectively observing my thoughts. It made it possible for me to put some distance between my impulses and acts, which helped me to better comprehend the fundamental reasons behind my behavior. I was able to develop the capacity to think things through before responding on impulse by engaging in mindfulness practices, which allowed me to interact with people in a more deliberate and compassionate manner.

Being honest about my background wasn't easy. It meant going back to painful and vulnerable times in the past, owning up to mistakes made, and taking accountability for their effects. But this trip to the core of my being provided me with deep realizations that accelerated my development.

An unexpected metamorphosis started as I faced these parts of myself. Realizing how I behaved had a profound effect on every area of my life. I replaced my self-criticism with understanding as I developed a renewed sense of self-awareness and self-compassion. This freeing change in viewpoint made it possible for me to accept my flaws as necessary building blocks for improvement.

Recognizing the complex network of my actions gave me the ability to steer clear of it. In instances where my narcissistic qualities were stoked in the past, I began to set boundaries, identify triggers, and employ coping methods. I was able to control my reactions better by proactively addressing these triggers, which led to healthier and deeper interactions.

This self-examination trip was life-changing. It was about changing my perspective on life, not just trying to analyze my conduct. It gave me a sense of responsibility and a dedication to lifelong learning.

As I proceed down this path, I see that introspection is a continuous process—a never-ending quest for personal development. There are new opportunities every day to develop empathy, sincerity, and sincere connections while learning more about myself and others.

Embracing Vulnerability: Learning the strength in vulnerability and its role in genuine connections.

Vulnerability felt, for the longest time, like a weakness I had to hide. It felt like a way to call attention to my shortcomings, something I felt would put my relationships in danger. I had no idea that being vulnerable would be essential to building real relationships.

My trip started off with me being reluctant to let anyone see behind the carefully manicured façade I had created. I covered up my fears with a façade of confidence because I was scared that people would think less of me if they saw my flaws. But this façade was a wall, impeding sincere intimacy and real ties.

During a heart-to-heart talk with my closest friend, Alex, it was a turning point. Alex reacted with kindness and understanding as I expressed my worries and hesitations, fearing criticism or distancing myself. My preconceived views that vulnerability is a weakness were dispelled by his ability to relate to my insecurities and provide support without passing judgment.

This incident led to a paradigm change. I came to see that showing vulnerability was an indication of bravery and sincerity rather than weakness. It served as a bridge that opened doors to more meaningful relationships by allowing people to see the true, unadulterated me.

I began little in order to embrace vulnerability even more. I confided in close friends about my anxieties, insecurities, and personal stories. I encountered understanding and acceptance rather than rejection. By making room for reciprocation, opening up promoted a relationship based on trust and vulnerability.

Furthermore, being vulnerable went beyond words. Its power was revealed to me in nonverbal cues: the unsaid vulnerability expressed by sympathetic body language, focused listening, and sincere emotional presence. These nuances strengthened ties and created ties that were more profound than words could express.

Vulnerability crept into my work life over time. I discovered that seeking collaboration and being transparent about uncertainties promoted an innovative and open atmosphere in team situations. It fostered a sense of community and camaraderie by fostering an atmosphere in which team members felt comfortable sharing thoughts and worries.

I became more and more aware of vulnerability's transformational power as I learned to embrace it. It was about being open to others' vulnerabilities as much as it was about exposing one's own. It came naturally to listen to them without passing judgment, to give them space to express their feelings, and to offer support.

I gained a new strength through vulnerability: the fortitude to be who I truly am, warts and all. It made it possible for me to develop more genuine relationships where being vulnerable was welcomed rather than avoided.

I discovered the deepest connections during these unfiltered times of genuineness. My carefully constructed walls came down, making room for partnerships based on sincere compassion and understanding.

Accepting vulnerability served as a spur for development on a personal level. It made clear the way to developing self-acceptance and self-compassion, which promotes resilience in the face of difficulties.

Ultimately, vulnerability became a superpower rather than a disadvantage. It was the secret to opening the door to real friendships and creating deep bonds that were enhanced by empathy and genuineness.

Chapter 3: Strategies for Change

Mindfulness Practices: Implementing mindfulness techniques for self-regulation and empathy.

My path to mindfulness started in the midst of a hectic, fast-paced life where stress and impatience seemed to be my constant companions. I had no idea that mindfulness could be so revolutionary in developing empathy and self-control until I happened onto it.

Practicing mindfulness at first seemed quite difficult. It seemed difficult to stop the maelstrom of ideas racing through my head while I sat in stillness. Nevertheless, I persevered, beginning with quick, guided meditation sessions. I eventually discovered how to watch my thoughts without becoming sucked into them, which gave me some measure of control over my rushing mind.

Being mindful turned into a regular routine and a haven from the chaos. It was in these quiet times that I learned to control myself. I discovered how to put some distance between the trigger and my response, as opposed to responding rashly to difficult circumstances. I was able to evaluate my feelings during this break and choose thoughtful, measured responses over impetuous outbursts.

Furthermore, awareness functioned as a mirror reflecting my emotional terrain. Rather than repressing or ignoring my discomfort, it enabled me to recognize it and sit with it. I was able to cultivate empathy by gaining a better understanding of both my own and other people's experiences by accepting these feelings without passing judgment.

A key example demonstrated the transforming ability of mindfulness to promote empathy. I noticed that my feelings were getting worse during a tense conversation with a coworker. Rather than giving in to my wrath at that moment, I stopped, inhaled deeply, and anchored myself in the here and now. I was able to change my perspective and see the underlying stress and worries behind my colleague's remarks thanks to this brief mindfulness period. I eased the tension and promoted mutual respect by approaching the conversation with empathy.

My life was full of mindfulness; it wasn't limited to my meditation practices. I made mindfulness a part of my everyday routine by identifying moments of awareness in ordinary tasks like doing the dishes or going for a walk, as well as by being completely present during discussions and enjoying meals without interruptions.

There was a noticeable change in my interactions as mindfulness crept in. Hearing words became only one aspect of listening; another was comprehending the feelings that underlie them. I was able to show true empathy by paying close attention and being really present, accepting other people's experiences without passing judgment or having any preconceived ideas.

Additionally, mindfulness served as a stabilizing force during tense situations. Rather than being carried away by the current wave of fear or anxiety, I grounded myself in the here and now by finding comfort in my breathing.

I learned about the mutually beneficial relationship between empathy and self-regulation through mindfulness. The capacity to control one's emotions made it easier to see other people's feelings, which led to the development of deeper relationships based on sincere empathy and understanding.

In summary, mindfulness evolved into a way of life rather than just a practice. It helped me develop self-control, which gave me the ability to react thoughtfully, and empathy, which improved my relationships by helping me comprehend other people's perspectives more fully.

Developing Empathy: Exercises to nurture empathy and understanding towards others.

I started my path to developing empathy with a straightforward but incredibly powerful exercise: active listening without judgment. It was an easy assignment at first, but it opened up levels of compassion and understanding that changed the way I saw and interacted with people.

Active listening seems foreign to me at first. During talks, I would frequently find myself forming opinions or answers rather than paying attention to what the other person was saying. But I made a commitment to improve, concentrating on giving conversations my whole attention.

The secret was to let go of my assumptions and really immerse myself in the speaker's story. I tried to decipher the underlying emotions behind their words by observing not only their body language but also their emotions.

I remember clearly having a talk with a friend of mine named Sara about a difficult issue she was facing at work. I listened intently, affirming her feelings and creating a safe environment for her to express herself, rather than giving advice or directing the topic toward my own experiences. I was able to better understand Sara's point of view through this active listening practice, which strengthened our relationship and encouraged empathy.

Perspective-taking was another activity that greatly aided in the development of empathy. I made a conscious effort to understand other people's perspectives and tried to put myself in their shoes. I had to accept a wider awareness of other people's perspectives and put aside my personal opinion in order to complete this activity.

An argument at a team meeting led to an eye-opening encounter. Rather than angrily arguing my point of view, I took a moment to consider my colleague's point of view. This change made it possible for me to understand their goals and concerns, which opened the door to a solution that took into account both points of view. Through this exercise, tensions were reduced and respect and cooperation were enhanced.

Additionally, journaling about empathy became a crucial part of my daily practice. Every day at the end, I thought back on the exchanges in which I tried to comprehend the thoughts and feelings of other people. Writing about these encounters made it clearer how important empathy is and how it affects the development of stronger ties.

Participating in voluntary activity gave developing empathy a useful context. I encountered a variety of people and their challenges while volunteering at a nearby shelter. Engaging with people who are experiencing hardships helped me develop a strong sense of empathy and reaffirmed the belief that every person has distinct experiences and feelings that should be understood and treated with kindness.

I also looked into the concept of random acts of kindness. Small deeds of kindness, lending a sympathetic ear to a stranger, or giving help without asking anything in return are examples of actions that cultivate empathy by promoting a sense of interconnectedness and shared humanity.

Through these activities, empathy became more than just a concept for me; it became a crucial component of my interactions. It changed the way I saw and interacted with the world, encouraging more meaningful relationships founded in sincere comprehension and compassion.

Chapter 4: Building Authentic Connections

Communication Redefined: Techniques for effective and empathetic communication.

In my past life, communication was a complex web of miscommunications and lost opportunities. I didn't realize the transformational power of actual connection through productive contact until I dove into the field of sympathetic communication.

Active listening was one essential tactic that completely changed the way I communicated. It turned into the main topic of my discussions. I started genuinely taking in the speaker's message—both spoken and unspoken—instead of just hearing words. Keeping eye contact, nodding affirmatively, and pausing before answering were all part of this exercise. Exchanges were transformed when one person listened intently, giving the other person a sense of value and being heard.

During a chat with my sibling, there was a crucial instance that demonstrated the need for active listening. Rather than offering my thoughts or suggestions, I concentrated on getting to know their feelings and worries. They valued being truly heard and understood, thus this strategy produced a deep relationship.

Additionally, it was found that asking open-ended questions was helpful in promoting sympathetic dialogue. I started asking questions that enabled the speaker to express their thoughts and emotions more thoroughly, as opposed to closed queries that only receive cursory answers. By probing deeply into their thoughts, feelings, and experiences, these questions hoped to spark stimulating dialogues that cultivated empathy.

During a difficult project, there is one specific occasion that comes to mind: I asked a coworker open-ended questions. Rather than presuming to know about their challenges, I encouraged them to express their worries by asking thoughtful questions. This method created a foundation of trust and understanding in addition to offering clarity.

Effective empathetic communication can now also be communicated nonverbally. I discovered how crucial tone, facial expressions, and body language are to enhancing spoken communication. By demonstrating empathy with nonverbal signs like keeping an open posture, grinning softly, or making comforting gestures, one can enhance the communication process and establish a stronger sense of connection.

Furthermore, the act of acknowledging and validating emotions during discussions played a crucial role in fostering compassionate communication. I addressed and validated someone's feelings rather than downplaying or trivializing them. The mutual understanding and support that resulted from this affirmation strengthened the friendship by establishing a secure space for honest expression.

The introduction of compassionate language was also a major factor in the transformation of communication. I made a conscious effort to swap out critical or dismissive language with kind remarks that expressed sympathy and support. This change in vocabulary fostered a climate in which connections strengthened and empathy blossomed.

With the help of these methods, communication changed from being a simple verbal exchange to a forum for sincere interactions. Understanding others' feelings, viewpoints, and experiences through empathetic communication helped to build relationships based on sincerity, trust, and empathy.

Cultivating Meaningful Relationships: Steps to foster genuine connections with others.

Amidst a world full of superficial exchanges, I was desperate for real relationships that went beyond casual acquaintanceship. It required intentional actions and reflection to find the way to building real connections with other people.

Self-awareness was the foundation for building real friendships. Knowing who I was, what I stood for, and what I wanted became crucial. I was able to show the world who I really am because of this self-discovery journey, which created the foundation for deep connections.

At a networking event, something unexpected happened. I revealed my own flaws and interests rather than putting on a polished front. Others were moved by this honesty, which opened the door for relationships based on sincerity and similar beliefs.

As the next critical phase, active presence became apparent. I learnt to be totally present in each interaction rather than just float through them. This deliberate presence created the foundation for deeper connections, whether it was through uninterrupted conversations or keeping eye contact.

Talking candidly with a new acquaintance at a heart-to-heart was a pivotal moment that demonstrated the significance of active presence. I established an environment where vulnerability and authenticity thrived by concentrating only on our talk and avoiding other distractions. This allowed us to build a connection based on sincere comprehension and empathy.

Real connections were fostered in large part by embracing vulnerability. Transparency regarding one's worries, desires, and past experiences facilitated deeper emotional bonds and mutual sharing. This openness demonstrated sincerity and encouraged others to follow suit, fostering relationships that went beyond surface-level interactions. A turning point occurred when I opened up to a coworker about my vulnerability. My candor inspired them to do the same, building a genuine bond based on mutual trust and understanding rather than making them dread judgment.

Furthermore, the art of active listening evolved to become a crucial component in developing sincere relationships. I focused on getting the speaker's feelings and points of view instead of waiting for my turn to speak. This sympathetic approach created an environment that encouraged more in-depth discussions and closer ties.

Empathy training was another essential component of developing real friendships. Mutual respect and caring relationships were fostered by acknowledging and recognizing the emotions of others, providing assistance without passing judgment, and being there for them through their highs and lows.

An eye-opening event occurred when a buddy needed comfort during a difficult time. Rather than making recommendations, I listened to them sympathetically and validated their feelings. Our friendship was strengthened by this empathetic deed, which promoted sincere support and understanding.

Finally, it should be noted that developing real connections requires reflection, genuineness, active presence, vulnerability, active listening, and empathy. Every move I took was a conscious decision to foster relationships that went beyond casual exchanges and filled my life with genuine, empathetic, and mutually understanding partnerships.

Chapter 5: Sustaining Growth

Daily Habits for Transformation: Incorporating daily practices to sustain personal development.

Maintaining personal growth and change required constant commitment, weaved into routines that served as the cornerstone of my journey of development. These regular routines were the threads that woven my life's metamorphosis together.

We started the day with a contemplative minute. I set aside time for meditation before the hustle started. This exercise helped me to stay grounded in the here and now and created a positive outlook for the day. It helped me maintain focus and clarity in the middle of life's chaos and welcomed the day with a clear head.

After that, journaling developed into a haven for introspection. I wrote down my aims, affirmations, and feelings of thankfulness every morning. Throughout the day, my actions and decisions were guided by this self-reflection technique, which gave me insight into my feelings, objectives, and places for progress.

Sustained progress required integrating learning into everyday activities. Whether it was through podcasts, online courses, or reading, I made time every day to increase my knowledge. This dedication to education fostered a growth attitude, extending horizons and promoting individual growth.

Setting daily goals was a crucial technique in maintaining transformation. These were modest, attainable goals rather than lofty aspirations. These daily objectives gave me a sense of success, whether it was finishing a book chapter or learning a new skill, and they inspired me to continue on my transformational journey.

In addition, maintaining one's physical health became essential to ongoing personal development. Regular exercise, be it a vigorous workout, a brisk walk, or yoga, energized the body and the mind. This regimen cultivated energy and discipline, supporting a holistic approach to personal growth.

In addition, little periods of introspection spaced throughout the day served as pillars for long-term development. Making quick assessments of one's feelings, behaviors, and responses led to self-awareness and clarity. These breaks acted as benchmarks to make sure my goals and ideals were being met.

Building relationships was an essential part of my everyday routine. Small acts of kindness, such as thank-you notes or spending time with close ones, can create a supportive environment that is essential for personal development.

The evening served as a reminder to take care of oneself and ponder. It became routine for me to partake in things that lifted my spirits, like reading, writing, or taking up a pastime. This calming ritual helped me get the good night's sleep and refreshment I needed for continued development.

To sum up, maintaining personal development requires a variety of everyday activities. Every ritual—whether it was self-care, journaling, studying, exercising, establishing goals, meditation, or time for introspection—contributed to the fabric of ongoing development.

These routines developed into essential parts of my identity and journey, not just routines. They served as the framework for constant change, making sure that personal development was a journey that was integrated into day-to-day activities rather than a destination.

Navigating Challenges: Strategies to overcome setbacks and continue on the path of growth.

Setbacks weren't obstacles on the path of human development; rather, they were crucial times for resiliency and learning. Overcoming these challenges required me to develop a toolkit of techniques that, in trying times, served as guiding lights and helped me progress along the path of development.

Adopting a change in perspective was the first tactic for dealing with obstacles. I reframed losses as chances for learning and progress rather than seeing them as failures. This shift in viewpoint gave me the ability to learn from hardship and tackle problems with hope and perseverance.

This change was best shown by a situation in which a project I ardently supported didn't produce the desired outcomes. Rather than give in to discouragement, I analyzed the event and took away important lessons that helped me in my subsequent pursuits. This habit of reinterpreting failures as teaching opportunities helped me to keep improving. Resilience also turned into a key component in overcoming obstacles. Resilience requires accepting feelings without letting them control you. I was able to overcome difficulties by navigating setbacks with a balanced viewpoint thanks to this practice of emotional regulation.

Engaging in self-compassion practice was another essential tactic. Upon experiencing difficulties, I choose to embrace self-compassion and show myself warmth and understanding instead of self-criticism. This self-empathetic deed fostered resilience by giving the emotional strength to face obstacles head-on and persevere.

Furthermore, getting help was essential to overcoming obstacles. In trying circumstances, I sought support from professionals, mentors, and reliable friends. Their advice and viewpoint provided a new point of view, which gave me courage and inspiration to keep moving forward with my growth.

A turning point in my professional life occurred during a career setback. Rather than taking the setback personally, I went to a mentor for advice. Their direction and encouragement gave me clarity and confidence, which helped me move forward with newfound vigor.

Another important tactic that came to light was the discipline of adaptation. Setbacks frequently required tactics and plans to be flexible and adaptable. My ability to embrace change and adjust to novel situations enabled me to overcome obstacles with grace, leading to unexpected breakthroughs and personal development.

A pivotal period that demonstrated flexibility occurred amid a significant life change. Rather than opposing change, I welcomed it and modified my objectives and tactics to fit the brand-new situation. This adaptability helped me not only get over the setback but also found new avenues for personal development.

Over time, reflection became a crucial tool for overcoming obstacles. I was able to assess the setback, pinpoint areas for development, and create plans of action for upcoming difficulties by taking some time to reflect. I used this self-analysis as a compass to steer me in the direction of more development.

In summary, overcoming obstacles on the route to growth required a combination of resilience, self-compassion, adaptation, self-shifting thinking, and introspection. These tactics developed into more than just tools; they became my pillars of strength, enabling me to move past obstacles, building my resilience, and guaranteeing my ongoing development.